YOUR KNOWLEDGE HAS VALUE

- We will publish your bachelor's and
  master's thesis, essays and papers

- Your own eBook and book -
  sold worldwide in all relevant shops

- Earn money with each sale

Upload your text at www.GRIN.com
and publish for free

Lydia Einenkel

Aus der Reihe: e-fellows.net stipendiaten-wissen

e-fellows.net (Hrsg.)

Band 834

Christ – the End or the Goal of the Law?

An Exegetical Analysis of Romans 10:4 in Context

GRIN Verlag

Bibliografische Information der Deutschen Nationalbibliothek:

Die Deutsche Bibliothek verzeichnet diese Publikation in der Deutschen National-
bibliografie; detaillierte bibliografische Daten sind im Internet über http://dnb.d-
nb.de/ abrufbar.

Imprint:

Copyright © 2011 GRIN Verlag GmbH
Druck und Bindung: Books on Demand GmbH, Norderstedt Germany
ISBN: 978-3-656-53388-7

This book at GRIN:

http://www.grin.com/en/e-book/262929/christ-the-end-or-the-goal-of-the-law

GRIN - Your knowledge has value

Der GRIN Verlag publiziert seit 1998 wissenschaftliche Arbeiten von Studenten, Hochschullehrern und anderen Akademikern als eBook und gedrucktes Buch. Die Verlagswebsite www.grin.com ist die ideale Plattform zur Veröffentlichung von Hausarbeiten, Abschlussarbeiten, wissenschaftlichen Aufsätzen, Dissertationen und Fachbüchern.

Visit us on the internet:

http://www.grin.com/

http://www.facebook.com/grincom

http://www.twitter.com/grin_com

The University of Edinburgh
   School of Divinity

Seminar: Writings of the Apostle Paul

Christ – the End or the Goal of the Law?
An Exegetical Analysis of Romans 10:4 in Context.

Vorgelegt von: Lydia Einenkel
Studiengang: Religious Studies and Theology

Semester: 2. FS

Datum: 17.04.2011

Christ – the End or the Goal of the Law?
An Exegetical Analysis of Romans 10:4 in Context.

Table of Contents

1. Introduction

The verse 10:4a "For Christ is the end of the law" (RSV) in Paul's Epistle to the Romans is a striking statement that needs to be considered carefully. In traditional Protestant, especially Lutheran, theology, it served along with Rom 3:28 the purpose of proving the huge gap between the (works of the) law and faith, or more exactly between justification through (works of the) law and faith in Christ.[1] It is still considered as "one of Paul's most provocative [. . .] statements"[2]. Putting aside these traditional prejudgments, I will look at the verse in the context of the whole epistle to the Romans, and try to answer the question what it means when Paul writes that Christ is the end of the law. Is there no law any more after Christ? What is this law? Is the law something bad so that Christ had to stop its existence?

2. Structural place

Our verse is to be found in the longest and probably youngest of the Pauline epistles, the Epistle to the Romans, which contains the treatment of the topics of Jewish-Gentile relations, righteousness or justification, faith and (less theological) practical ethical issues as well as Paul's plan for the Jerusalem collection. It is located at the very heart of Romans 9--11, which thematises Israel and its position in the *göttlichen Heilsplan*. Within Romans 9-11 the statement we are considering must be seen as part of 9:30-10:21, where Paul shows how God now offers to the Gentiles the uprightness promised first to Israel.[3]

More precisely, the statement is in the closing verse of the pericope Romans 10:1-4. Paul expresses here his desire for the saving of the Jews. Though having a "zeal for God" (10:2) they "did not submit to God's righteousness" (10:3). Immediately after that follows verse 10:4, which is connected to the previous one with *gar* ("for"). That makes clear that they should be read together. Vv. 5ff. are also connected with *gar*. But I consider them as loosely connected, for the topic is still righteousness and law but with the reference to Moses a new argument starts.[4] The closest reading of "end of law" is of course within the whole verse 10:4;

---

[1] For a brief overview on the history of exegesis see: Charles E. B. Cranfield, *The Epistle to the Romans 9-16* (ICC; Edinburgh: T&T Clark, 1979), 515-18.

[2] Steven R. Bechtler. "Christ, the Telos of the Law: The Goal of Romans 10:4," *CBQ* 56 (1994): 288.

[3] John L. Lodge, *Romans 9-11: A Reader-Response Analysis.* (ISfCJ 6; Atlanta: Scholars Press, 1996), 115.

[4] Because of the causal dependence (*gar*) of each of the verses in Rom 10:1-4 I regard them as one pericope with 10:4 as the final verse. (James D.G. Dunn, *Romans 9-16.* (WBC 38b; Dallas: Word Publisher, 1988), 578; Ernst Käsemann, *An die Römer.* (HNT; Tübingen: J.C.B. Mohr, 1980⁴), 270; Lodge, *Romans*, 102; Bechtler, *Christ*, 288; Joseph A. Fitzmeyer, *Romans: A New Translation with Introduction and Commentary.* (AB 33; NY: Doubleday, 1993), 581; Robert Jewett, *Romans: A Commentary.* (HERM; Minneapolis: Fortress Press, 2007), 606. However, this is not a consensus at all for a lot of commentators see 10:4 as the starting verse connected with 10:5ff (Karl Barth, *Der Römerbrief.* (Zürich: EVZ-Verlag, 1919), 300; George E. Howard, "Christ the End of the Law: The Meaning of Romans 10 4 ff.," *JBL* (88 1969), 336) or they do not even consider a turn from 10:4 to 10:5ff at all (John Murray, *The Epistle to the Romans* Part 2. (LCNT; London: Marshall, Morgan &

that means not just to consider the first half in isolation but also in connection with the second half of the verse. Romans 10:4a forms a unit with the statement: "that everyone who has faith may be justified" (10:4b).

3. Topic

The verse is about the law and Christ and in particular their relationship to each other. So in a broader sense it thematises the transition from the Jewish understanding of serving God and the change which came with Christ. Are the law and Christ contradictions? Is Christ against the law so that it is ended? The second part of the verse gives a detailed explanation of the statement that Christ is the end of the law. The goal is justification for the believers.

4. Concerns, questions, emphasis

Among the questions this paragraph raises are: what does Paul mean by *telos nomou*? What is *nomos* for Paul here? What is the meaning of *telos*? Why do we find this sentence especially in this place in the epistle? And, once we have decided for one reading, how does that fit to the other statements in Romans about law and faith, and what impact does this verse have?

5. Analysis

5.1 LANGUAGE AND KEY WORDS

There are no textual variants listed in Nestle-Aland for Romans 10:4. A closer look to the language of this verse has to focus rather on the way how crucial words should be translated and therefore interpreted. This task seems to be not that difficult concerning *nomos,* which can mean 'law' and also 'custom'. It is contextually very clear that Paul has the law, especially the Jewish law (that is the Torah) in mind.[5] We come to that meaning because of the place of 10:4 within the whole epistle. As I have shown above, it is located in the middle of a passage which deals primarily with Israel and its law. It would be inconsistent to read in that context a general law apart from the Torah. Telos, however, has at least two possible meanings: 'end' and also 'target/goal' in the sense of fulfilment.[6] The translation of this word

---

Scott, 1967), 46; Leon Morris, *The Epistle to the Romans.* (Michigan: Grand Rapids, 1988), 377.; Charles K. Barrett, *A Commentary on the Epistle to the Romans.* (London: Black, 1991²), 182).

[5] For further information about the meaning of *nomos* in Romans 10:4 see: Fitzmeyer, *Romans*, 284; Howard, *Christ*, 331; Cranfield, *Romans*, 515f.

[6] Cranfield lists three possible meanings: 1. Fulfillment, 2. Goal, 3. Termination. I see goal and fulfilment as so closely connected that I regard them together as one reading. Cranfield, *Romans*, 516.

is very important for the understanding of this verse.[7] In the understanding that Christ is the *end* of the law, the law and Christ would be two contrary systems. The law has no *raison d'être* anymore and there is nothing good in it. But if Christ is the *goal* of the law,[8] that would mean that the law leads to Christ, that it is the purpose of the law to prepare and open the way to Christ. Therefore, the law is rather good and it had to be there all the time. But one needs to look closer at the context to understand Paul's view of the law as well as of the task of Christ to decide this question.

5.2 CONTEXTUAL ANALYSIS

In the following discussion, I will move from the most possible narrow context to the broadest, comprising the whole epistle.

5.2.1 ROMANS 10:4A WITHIN ROMANS 10:4

The first aspect which helps us to understand the statement that Christ is *telos nomou* is to analyze the term *dikaiousune*. In Romans 10:4 Paul gives us the result of Christ's being *telos nomou*: 'so that everyone who has faith may be justified'. Because of this very close, consecutive connection (*eis*), 'justification' seems to be an important item to find the sense of in Romans 10:4. Justification is for Paul not only forgiveness of sins (3:25; 4:7-8) but also, and more important, the inclusion of the whole world into the covenant or within God's people. We can see this in his stressing of the equality of Jews and Gentiles (1:16; 2:9-10; 3:9,22; 10:12) before God (and in the passages about the promise to Abraham and his descendents, 4:1--25; 9.6ff).

5.2.2 ROMANS 10:4A WITHIN ROMANS 10:1-4

Paul starts this pericope with an expression of his desire for the Jews (10:1). He gives the reason (*gar*) for that in the next verse: they have a zeal for God, although not enlightened (10:2). Why? For (*gar*) they tried to establish their own righteousness rather than the righteousness which comes from God, so that they did not submit to God's righteousness (10:3). The next verse, namely Romans 10:4, is also connected with *gar* – so Christ as the *telos* of the law is regarded as a reason for the statements before. One exegetical difficulty is here what Paul means with "own righteousness". If one reads "exclusive righteousness which

---

[7] But *telos* is certainly a noun and should not be read as a verb to stress the chosen interpretation as Snider does: "For Christ ends the law". Theodore M. Snider, *The Continuity of Salvation: A Study of Paul's Letter to the Romans (*North Carolina/London: McFarland Publishers, 1984), 130.
[8] For examples of the use of *telos* as goal in ancient Greek literature, see: Jewett, *Romans*, 619.

is only for the Israelites"[9] rather than "individual self-attained righteousness"[10], a probable connection to 10:4, reading *telos* as goal, becomes clear: Because the goal of the law is and has ever been Christ, i.e., the Christ-event for *all who believe*, Paul can criticise Jews when they seek their own exclusive righteousness.

> "The problem described in 10:3, therefore, is not that Israel, by its meritorious efforts, is attempting to create its own righteousness but that its zealous commitment to its exclusivistic view of the covenant precludes the possibility of God's offer of salvation to Gentiles outside the covenant. [...] In so doing, they exclude themselves from the grace God now offers in Christ."[11]

God's goal to which the Torah leads and which is realized in Christ is inclusion, not exclusion.

5.2.3 ROMANS 10:4A WITHIN ROMANS 1-16

The question of Paul's view of the relationship between the law and Christ can be seen in a broader sense. Since *nomos* is the Jewish law which was revealed by God to Israel, we might also ask for the connection between the Israel with its Scripture and the Gospel of Christ.[12] We find a first hint in Romans 1:2, where Paul says that God "promised beforehand [the Gospel] through his prophets in the Holy Scriptures". That shows very clearly the continuity from the Holy Scriptures and thus also from the law to the Gospel. The Gospel is further described as "the gospel concerning his Son" (Rom 1:3), so one can say that the coming of Christ was promised beforehand, and that means that there is a close connection between the "Old Testament"[13] and the Gospel. Another proof for the historical continuity in the revelation of God and in his plan for humankind is to be found in Romans 9:5. Paul speaks here about the Israelites of whose "race, according to the flesh" also Christ is (cf. 1:3). So there is a positive, teleological relationship between the "old covenant" and the new being in Christ. It is not something entirely new but the result of promises and the last step in God's plan (Rom 4). Christ stands as the goal in continuity to the law and the Israelites in terms of Scripture, genealogy and Salvation history.

---

[9] Mary A. Getty. "Paul and the Salvation of Israel: A Perspective on Romans 9-11," CBQ 50 (1988): 467; Howard, *Christ*, 336.

[10] So, e.g., Käsemann: „Es geht um die typisch jüdische, im zelos begründete, objektiv vorliegende Verfehlung." Käsemann, *Romans*, 271.

[11] Bechtler, *Christ*, 298.

[12] Leuba supports the view that *nomos* can mean next to "Torah" and more seldom "norm" or "rule" also "the Old Testament as a whole". J.L. Leuba, "Law," VB 227f.

[13] I put "Old Testament" in quotes to show the hesitation in using this term referring to Paul's time. Though the term goes indeed back to Paul (2Cor 3:14), I am aware of the anachronism for the Scripture in use at this time did not have the same content and order as we know it now. The process of canonization (or canonizations) was not finished.

Probably one of the most important purposes or outcomes of the law is for Paul that it leads to knowledge of sin (7:7). Therefore it plays a magnificent role in God's acting towards the world. Not before humans recognize that they are sinners or live under sin, can they put their faith and loyalty in Christ. Because of the sin of humans, Christ's life and death were necessary. So the law is indeed a good thing, since because of it came knowledge of the sin which led to the coming of Christ, who opened the opportunity of justification through faith for all human beings, including the gentiles. This is a very climactic understanding of salvation history. Within that, Christ is the fulfillment of the law. That is why he was promised beforehand (see above), and everything should have led to him from the beginning.

Besides this, the reading of *telos nomou* as "end of law" doesn't make really sense in the light of the many verses and passages in Paul's letter to the Romans where he speaks very positively about the law (e.g. 7:12). It would be utterly contradictory to write even only partly positively about the law if its end came with Christ.[14] We find first proofs for that in chapter 3 of Romans. First it speaks of the advantage of the Jew (3:1ff) and also Paul says in 3:31, interestingly, that by faith the law is not overthrown but upheld. How can the believers in Christ uphold the law by faith if it is already ended with Christ? Apparently, the law and Christ are not binary oppositions but a contentious flow, one (the law) leads to the other (Christ). By reading Romans this way, there is no possibility of the so often stated antithesis between righteousness through works of the law on the one hand and through faith on the other hand. Besides this, we find "no statement in any of Pauline epistles that Christ has abolished the law".[15]

---

[14] But on the other hand Dunn can read *telos* as "end" without seeing a contradiction to Paul's positive view on the law for he distinguishes strongly between the law and works of the law and of course by not defining the law as a way of earning righteousness. Dunn, Romans, 596-8.

[15] Cranfield, *Romans*, 519. Similiar: Lodge; *Romans*, 115.

6. Conclusion

Because of lexical and contextual considerations I clearly prefer the following reading of Romans 10:4:

"For Christ is the goal of the law for the justification of all who believe."

That means that Christ is the goal or the aim rather than the end in the sense of termination[16] of the law. This is to be seen as fulfillment. Nearly every statement concerning the law, Israel, the Jews or the prophets shows continuity to the gospel and Christ. This is not just an unidentified or random continuity but it is focused on salvation and justification. That means it is already written in the law that its goal is to transform the particular justification for Israel to the universal justification for all who believe.[17] Exactly that took place in the Christ-event. Thus, Christ is the goal of the law because through him God established the inclusion of the gentiles into God's people. God has not broken his covenant with Israel (11:1), rather he has widened it to the whole world as it was already the promise to Abraham. Further, the law leads to recognition of sin which one needs before one accepts the need of Christ and his death. The law is good; it leads to Christ as its goal.

Summa summarum, we can speak about a transformed continuity of God's way of salvation towards inclusion[18] in which Christ is the goal of the law. He is the climax in a long dramatic story, maybe a new chapter but not an independent new volume.

---

[16] Murray; *Romans*, 49-50.

[17] Especially Rom 9:25-26 speaks about the Inclusion prophesied in the Old Testament. Bechtler, *Christ*, 291.

[18] A lot of commentators regard "inclusion" as the main point in Romans 10:4 or a wider passage: Getty, *Paul*, 476; Howard, *Christ*, 336; Lodge, *Romans*, 116.

7. Bibliography

MONOGRAPHS

- Barrett, Charles K. *A Commentary on the Epistle to the Romans.* London: Black, 1991².

- Barth, Karl. *Der Römerbrief.* Zürich: EVZ-Verlag, 1919.

- Cranfield, Charles E. B. *The Epistle to the Romans 9-16.* Vol. 2 of *Romans.* The International Critical Commentary on the Holy Scriptures of the Old and New Testaments, Edinburgh: T&T Clark, 1979.

- Dunn, James D.G. *Romans 9-16.* Word Biblical Commentary 38b. Dallas: Word Publisher, 1988.

- Fitzmeyer, Joseph A. *Romans: A New Translation with Introduction and Commentary.* The Anchor Bible 33, NY: Doubleday, 1993.

- Jewett, Robert. *Romans: A Commentary.* Hermeineia – A Critical and Historical Commentary on the Bible, Minneapolis: Fortress Press, 2007.

- Käsemann, Ernst. *An die Römer.* Handbuch zum Neuen Testament. Tübingen: J.C.B. Mohr, 1980⁴.

- Lodge, John L. *Romans 9-11: A Reader-Response Analysis.* International Studies in formative Christianity and Judaism 6, Atlanta: Scholars Press, 1996.

- Morris, Leon. *The Epistle to the Romans.* Michigan: Grand Rapids, 1988.

- Murray, John. *The Epistle to the Romans* Part 2. The London Commentary on the New Testament, London: Marshall, Morgan & Scott, 1967.

- Snider, Theodore M. *The Continuity of Salvation: A Study of Paul's Letter to the Romans.* North Carolina/London: McFarland Publishers, 1984.

Journal Articles

- Bechtler, Steven R. "Christ, the Telos of the Law: The Goal of Romans 10:4." *The Catholic Biblical Quarterly* 56 (1994): 288-308.

- Getty, Mary A. "Paul and the Salvation of Israel: A Perspective on Romans 9-11." *The Catholic Biblical Quarterly* 50 (1988): 456-496.

- Howard, George E. "Christ the End of the Law: The Meaning of Romans 10 4 ff." *Journal of Biblical Literature* 88 (1969): 331-337.

Dictionaries

- von Allmen, J.J. Leuba, ed. *Vocabulary of the Bible.* London: Lutterworth Press, 1958.